LOVE and STRANGE HORSES

PITT POETRY SERIES

Ed Ochester, Editor

LOVE
and
STRANGE
HORSES

Nathalie Handal

UNIVERSITY OF PITTSBURGH PRESS

Published by the University of Pittsburgh Press, Pittsburgh, PA 15260
Copyright © 2010, Nathalie Handal
All rights reserved
Manufactured in the United States of America
Printed on acid-free paper
10 9 8 7 6 5 4 3 2 1
ISBN 13: 978-0-8229-6060-7
ISBN 10: 0-8229-6060-5

To Liam, Jason, Mai,
Sargon and Mahmoud

Here

     My steps along this street
resound
          in another street
in which
       I hear my steps
passing along this street
in which

Only the mist is real

                Octavio Paz

So I return to the words of Jorge Luis Borges that "myth is the beginning of literature, and also at its end." I return to Mahmoud Darwish: "She doesn't say: / Love is born a living creature / before it becomes an idea. / And I also don't say: / Love has become an idea / But it seems like it."

Contents

Pasaje

Who saw the jaguar by the lake?
Who saw grass grow on the bones of the living?
Who saw the wreaths of dark shadows?
Who longs for partings, dreads them?
Who longs for the rumination of birds?
Who belongs to time?
Who hunts for a nest then hunts for freedom?
Who lives in absence and rots in fever towers?
Who lives alone?
Who illuminates the voyage to the devil's flame?
Who accepts sex as the glory of the body, passion its companion?
Who understands love differently?
Who minds a mind that goes completely?
Who bows in order not to fall?
Who loses the world by the waters?
Who loses sound by the hours?
Who lives desolate and howling?
Who sees the eyes that have left a trail where the ground creaks?
Who knows the three movements of the heart: intima', erotica,
    terre música?

I

Movement One—Intima'

Like the moon, like death, like next week, the distant past is one of those things that can enrich ignorance. It is infinitely malleable and agreeable, far more obliging than the future and far less demanding of our efforts. It is the famous season favored by all mythologies. Who has not, at one time or another, played with thoughts of his ancestors, with the prehistory of his flesh and blood?

Jorge Luis Borges

Flames at Hurr Mountain

I

History has a way of
moving the heart backward.

A way of moving it forward
to protect its past, its tired mind.

Its deep stories. Dark angles.
The phobia it sculpts out of night.

It's not about a song.
It's about a ruin, a voice's fainting crescendo.

It's loud. It's narrow. It's quiet.
This is something we know—it stirs.

Stirs the branches of darkness. Stirs the
echoes of rivers. Stirs what is not ours.

And what's ours. Gone and gone.
Here and here, there and there.

II

The mountains hold words,
hold gods, hold flame.

Flame that distracts shadows,
and what stands behind them.

The mountains are high
and low, low and high.

Higher than we can find, like
a word impossible to grow.

A seed impossible to grow.
A glow impossible to stop.

An arrow impossible to stop.
A poison impossible to find.

Love impossible to find,
like that kiss that missed your lips.

Like the laughter cutting breath
in half to save itself a piece

of what still beats inside.
Alive as dead.

Dead and alive—
one bird after the other, chirping.

There is no God but God,
no desire but wind,

caught deep in a mountain
trying to rise to an earth that awaits

the opening of flames
we wish we'd seen before.

Brokenmusic

Maybe when you are ready for music
 every instrument around is broken
Maybe when you are ready for freedom
 your heart can no longer beat
Maybe when you grow madness
 you find what you were meant to see
Maybe if you show me
 how desire begs
play a tune in E minor
 the slow river of wings will
reveal itself.

But it had to come to this instead:
 a broken violin
 the heart, unsolved
 an argument with Jesus or Mohammed
 —exile has its ways.
 Now your breath is a flat tune
 limping its way around
 the wake of your mouth.

In the Ruins

Pero yo ya no soy yo
Ni mi casa es ya mi casa.

Federico García Lorca

He comes without her.

I ask him if he lives close to the sea now.
He says,
There is no water only water
no song only song
no version of death
I'm comfortable with.

I imagine his body against the waves
and a rock beside him, words tight around it.
There is no cry only cry
no view of Carmel only Carmel
no one around to listen.

Where is the country?
It seems useless to count
how long it's been since we've seen it.

He says nothing. And I wonder
why she didn't come—
had she forgotten
his name in Arabic?

I move toward him. Move to feel the light
against my dream, to feel what remains.

He is everywhere. Who is he now?
Who am I?
Have we found a dove,
an earth?
He is everywhere.
Then she arrives and she asks him,
Why are you here—
didn't I tell you to leave?
You did, he said, *but like you, I couldn't go.*

After Mahmoud Darwish

The Unnatural Apologies of Shadows

We say lightning has no wings
when it slides down our houses

We say loss is just a condition
we acquire to bury our pity further

We say the bleeding hands
on the table filled with red wine
imported products and passports
are just reminders of
who we have become

We have no titles no birthright
no groves or Shakespeare
to return to

We apologize for the fear
growing out of our ribs

Apologize for the numbers
still etched on our tongues

Listen, *Tonight*

to the leaves murmuring
in the yellow fields
to the aches of a peasant
the pain of an abandoned child
look at Tiberias disguised in shadows
at the miniscule footsteps of stars
feel the touch of a beggar

and answer me why we pretended—
when we measured the earth

and there was no space for both of us

Sun Moon Midnight

The road has seven circles of sun drawn onto its chest.

That's what happens when we lose focus.

We lose the way.

Find ourselves in a place we will hate remembering.

It's about absence.

That iron cell inside us.

Or perhaps it's about the night swallowing
what we leave of desire on its black handkerchiefs.

We pass windows of inferno:
a one-legged woman nude on a satin sheet,
a moldy closet with dead dandelions,
an angel with her heart beside her,
a maiden with her hair cut off.
In a midnight abandoned by the moon,
we tell ourselves we aren't meant to know everything.

Of the End

there they were
the hours I left
there they were
the whispers I stepped on accidentally
there they were
the men I never undressed for
there they were
the places I said
I'd return to   to understand myself
there they were
the letters, ladders, lamps, lizards, suede gloves
the arrows, canaries, rivers, braziers, ropes, foxes,
the piano piano piano
the letters (did I say that already)

there they all were—
that's what it feels like inside—
nine hunched wings and nothing to see

The Hawk Quartet

I

You greet me only with your eyes.
That evening you write to me
on a starless night,
I imagine my response—
I never write back.

II

Years later, we meet. We try
to say something but don't.
One month later, you drown yourself
in a tunnel of red.

III

Another year passes.
While on a train,
the sky hiding pleas,
I share a seat with a man you loved,
between us a crack, beside us a window of hard tears
and for a second, I hear the roar you hid under the chair.

IV

Months later, sheets of paper,
like a limping movement, slip from the table
slowly to the cement floor.

I pick one up and there I find your note,
your final line,
I follow birds that either migrate or prey. And you?

I sit to write but find nothing—
like a hawk unable to find its quartet
even in his stink—
only loneliness can understand.

The Map of Home

Is there a new lover in your bed tonight
I ask

Where are your lips tonight
I ask

Where is your shame tonight
and your white tulips your gun
your olive branches

Where is the evening
and the question
you once had the courage to ask
about who my father was
under the rain

Where are you stationed tonight
is your heart beating and why

Who are you tonight

Is there love in your bed
I ask

Suddenly his hand falls over my mouth
that's what happens in conflicts

Butterfly, or What Is Unnamed

Paint my face the color of your revolt,
    drive through ice storms,
hide your knife under the white curtain,
    hold my breath with your eyes,
slide your hands in my pants
    while you watch grass grow.

Do what I say:
    behind the row of blue moons
is a tin cup.
    Pick it up.

Unstrung Lute

You play with the hem of my dress,
shut the windows,
stand in front of a row of shoes
and count the faces you will never see again:
a body of holes,
small saints,
a river of red ribbons.
What use is love to us now?
Instead, let me take a picture of you.

Country of Days

Day One

He made love all afternoon,
forgot about it the next day.

Day Two

He thought,
what's faith if not broken love,
to sleep in another's crossing.

Day Three

He said,
Give me your gun, Joel,
it's Oklahoma.

And I thought,
what would Allen Ginsberg have told him,
Sugar, you ain't nothing but trash.

We both turn around
to see if Jesus is standing behind us.

Day Nine

Rising out of this dark
an unshakable glory.

Don't Believe

Believe in the color of water,
in the dance-wings.
Believe in the season's hard kiss,
in the weaver's reverie.
Believe in the glow of drizzle,
in the fire-well,
in the blueberry field,
in the direction of your hands.
Believe in what you gave,
heavy sorrow,
stolen jazz,
hurting feet.
Believe in the fever-deep pale street.
Believe in the divided breaths of untitled men
and wait for the torture to believe in you.

Autobiography of Night

I refuse my darkness,
    tunes and uncertainty.
I ask any question
    to forget what I'm not able to ask,
to forget that I listened to the devil
    and the rain, and it was a sound
I didn't want to recognize—
    its drops too light, graceful,
reminding me of the ghosts between my sheets,
    the empty closets of my divided hour,
the walls, the peeling paint,
    the barbed wire, a view of my history,
of all that I've been blind to,
    a view of the marble floor I keep
crying on, and the bird I hold against my grief.
    Confess, a voice asks. Did the passing sparrow in your sleep
tell you what you wanted to ask? Did you feel your navel
    pressed against the earth, asking, *do we*
continue to live with the one we think we love
    when nothing else means something to us?
Confess.

Pendule

He walks without a coat.
He drinks beer
or is it wine?
He takes his fedora off
or is it a panama?
He speaks in French
or is it Spanish?
He saves the air
in the middle of his throat
or is it a small message?
He says, *She and I*
forgot the line
we wrote to each other—
the closest we've been to love
or perhaps
We didn't mean
to ignore each other
we just forgot.

Intermisión

I don't know if I left the window open,
or the electric fireplace on,
not sure if my name is Natalya or Navarro,
but I vaguely remember
someone calling me by one of those names.
No one found the book
Octavio Paz dedicated to me
or the notes I wrote about
the streets of Mexico City
and the person I once was
three blocks away from the taquería.
Who can explain intermissions—
they come to your life
without warning and all you can do
is wait until it's time to start again.
Meanwhile, I feel the heat burning
on the tip of my hip—
a feeling shivering electric
on the flesh, the fever of what
I no longer know.

Akhmatova and I: Boleros

How much gloom in your love,
and why does this trickle of blood
irritate the petal on your cheek?

Anna Akhmatova, *Poem Without a Hero*

I ask: if I start digging the red soil
for wounds, what else will I find?

She says: yourself, on the shoulders of a cliff,
looking at the same patch of sky
that has held the agitation of your wings
and the person you didn't hold closer.

I ask: what do you remember most?

She says: when he comes to me
as if I'm the only woman he has ever kissed
and I accept the wreckage that follows
so that his lips stay close to mine.

I tell her: just imagine cherries against arrows.
Just imagine rows of orchids, willows, honeysuckle.
Just imagine petals behind petals beside petals,
the ripples of a lake, the lament of a hidden face,
purple nights, dying buds, rustling leaves,
just imagine—that's what happens
when love turns wild in a dream.

She says: have you ever danced a bolero?

History by Candlelight

When we listened to birds chirping
early in the Caribbean mornings,

when we found out that
a kiss was like water slapping against bare feet,

when by candlelight you touched
that part of me that wanted you most
and a door flung open like the year
that couldn't wait any longer

we held each other
and turned the small humming
of furious beats deep in the heart
into who we are meant to be.

Love and Strange Horses—*Intima'*

.— •

One hundred breaths split the air
as I lean
on the only pine tree I find.
It's early or late, it's breezy or hot.
The fields are dry. Summer is near.
The horses are everywhere,
strangely galloping a dream,
but I can't remember
how to call them,
so I stand back, watch them pass.

.— ١

The first time I rode a horse
my body found the music of fire,
crackling the wind. An unbearable pleasure
that also left me with a burn on the side of my leg.
A sign, the horsekeeper told me, *of longing.*
A need to return—to belong.
After all, departure is like
pushing the weight of our heart
against the village
whose name has kept us awake.

.— ٢

Rafael came from somewhere in Eurasia.
I passed my hands through his mane—

saw a history of conquests and battles,
a field of hay, a mount of truth,
heard a silent ring,
his eyes asking me to go with him,
to confess something sacred,
to name something lustful.
Nothing of where he came from,
or who I was, disturbed us.

.— ٣

I knew he was different by the way he ran—
without pause,
without grace,
without distraction,
without ease.
He was told how to move in the world
and resented it.
He knew he would never own anything.

.— ٤

He came toward me.
It was a quiet afternoon.
I stood unmoving.
And we listened to the untitled music
circling the earth like an anthem
free of its nation.

.— ٥

He was unfamiliar to me,
approaching as if he possessed the land.
Every morning he stopped five feet
from the river.

He waited for the light
to touch the leaves,
waited for me to look away
before he disappeared.
One day he stopped coming,
I assumed he had finished burying all he needed to
five feet away from the water.

.— ٦

Darkness has no shape except
the one you give it, he told me.
And handed me
an apple, an orange, a lily,
and a basket of grapes.
I said, *Are these the shape of darkness*
or a distraction the heart needs?

.— ٧

One day, as the horses passed by,
one left a strangeness inside me.

.— ٨

The stranger he became
the stronger his memory grew inside me.
That's the thing about love,
it likes to leave its mark
while counting birds in reverse.
It's about belonging, it whispers, *intima'.*
I suppose we need evidence of desire—
to have broken a heart in this dangerous world;
evidence that we belonged somewhere once.

II

Movement Two—Elegía Erótica

L'impossible est la seule image qui puisse satisfaire celui qui la contemple.

François Jacqmin

Les Fenêtres—Three Drafts

Draft One

Say *hello. What's your name?*
Place a thought in his mouth.
Whisper you want him—immediately.
Say, *baby you smell like no other.*
And as he enters, leave.

Draft Two

Look at him. But don't greet him.
Leave your coffee breath as is.
Don't speak.
Lower your eyes. You're not
interested. Then stand up,
motion—*follow me.* And as he enters,
enter too. But don't let him know.

Draft Three

Stand naked with heels on.
Ask him to kiss your belly button.
To turn his breathing the other way,
and decide which way to enter.

Corriendo

Let's say
   you took sea salt
      and placed it on my lips

Let's say
   by midday you told me your
      famous lyrics aren't written by you

Let's say
   your heart bleeds on my hands
      and you say someone else's name
      while inside

Let's say you show me your dangerous eyes
   your hard smile
      your other side, steep and wide

Let's say you bring me to the scent of lust
   and let the sun fall between our legs
      would that be enough
      or isn't love stranger.

Ahmad

When you come I will ask,
what waits behind your door?
You will go far into my eyes.
What divides your heartbeats?
You will take my hands.

When you come
the shadow of your eyes
slanted against dawn
will pray seven times,
seven times prayer will return
in small echoes.

When you come
we will count the kites
flying above the field,
you will put your face on my hands,
look at me, as if I were away for too long.

When you come
a current will run through our chills,
God will arrive seven times,
seven times
we will not see his face.

You are burning inside my mind
like nothing else I've known.
When are you coming?

Je suis déjà venu.
Did you really?
Bien sûr.
Touch me.
Mais je te touche.
Kiss me.
Regarde tes lèvres, elles sont miennes.
Listen to me.
Habibti.
I say your name softly,
Ahmad Ahmad
to disturb the loneliness.

Elephant Fever

The strained horseman and I waited

for a back room, for a glass of whiskey
to be poured on our swollen fingers,

waited for the cooling engine outside,

the morning details gathering testaments

but it was too late—

there was an elephant in front of us
like a fever too deep to cool.

It was late,

I was strangely stranded between his legs,

and he had faith in what deceived him.

Entrances and Other Endings

1—

Your chest against me. Your lament against me. Your tears against me. Your angst against me. Your sudden laughter against me. A possible relief. A sliding into. An unbuttoning of lust. Nevermind. It's only the you I want to witness. I risk your touch tapping my heart. I count your name count. The tapping of your fingers against my leg. The numbness of our hands. And the piling up of bones against our kiss.

2—

You are as desirable as you think. When you pull me closer I see what I would not miss. It's a slow burning of ash against ash. It's your breath unfastening my blouse. Your eyes giving me providence. I keep your face in a safe place. Hope to see it again when the knots in your body have tied the strings to your throat. Darling, you are a song unkissed, an ocean older than the ruins of a cherub. You are that dark I threw away long before I found the way out.

3—

Before I saw a seesaw of shadows against water. Before an empire of smoking shade stationed themselves in memory. Before the light paused on rooftops, I saw a deer or was it a dragon? Saw a fern or was it an icon? I subtracted the hums from the song. Waited for you, railroad track after railroad track. I even took your telescope, in hope of finding anything that belongs to you: your leather shoes, your pink thorns.

Javier

Javier gave me a rose. The next day Juanita had the same rose. The day after, the rose was on the lieutenant's desk. In the afternoon the rose was on Mathida's bed table. When I returned to my room, the rose was no longer there. I saw Javier. I never said anything. But by the way he looked at me, I knew there was something we were both going to miss.

I opened the windows to the Zocalo and asked Javier to
stand behind me, as in a movie that we both hated but
kept watching because we needed the love scenes, needed
to see voices when we touched each other, needed to hear
the debates of others so that we didn't hear our own. I
asked him, Did you have a lonely childhood? Kill a horse?
Marry a shadow? I asked him, Can I suck your nipple or
are you suppose to be sucking mine? He said, *mujer*—
because he never called me by my name—turn around;
the pages of silence can hold only one of us.

Amor, donde esta la ventana? And why are your lips swollen, the back of your knees tattooed? Let me worry about unbuttoning your pants, let me worry about where you will sleep, you on the sofa, I in your dreams; you in my dreams, I on the sofa. You see we spoke better when we were where the other once was. *Amor,* you see, since we picked the wrong God to pray to, here we are on Avenida Juárez, staring at a photo of Magdalena and still praying we could stop licking lust out of each other.

It was a day when cockroaches and beer plead for space with the phantoms in the room. The day Javier and I lay with an unsigned paper between us, when "La Malagueña" was playing but we could not sing along. We had grown deaf of voice, song, melody. We had grown unamused by the icons in our books, by speeches presidents and lovers gave. We needed to get back to the night when he invited me out, said *Caballero, dos palomas y un vino rojo*—Jubileo de Guadalupe, Baja, Mexico—*por favor*. When he took my closeness off, smelled my body as if he was looking for mercy, we went somewhere together, unbroken.

He undid my corset, asked for two kisses; he wanted both of me—the one I show and the one I hide. Perhaps I didn't understand so I moved closer, his lips full. I wanted to see something else but I didn't ask. Then another woman came in the room. He opened her eyes and her blouse, closed his eyes and my shirt. Here we were, the three of us, uncovered—not knowing if her arrival meant our departure, or if departure was not knowing when we were dressed or undressed.

Javier bought a tamarindo, I bought a manzana. We both blamed each other, then counted the lemons for tequila. It was a ritual, or a prayer session we did instead of singing "Ave Maria." *Dios* is with us, except when we are sober. You see, we discovered, Javier and I, that since hunger is difficult to get rid of, why not learn to say verses when everything around us is clear: a bare room, a mattress, a window, two tequila glasses? We understood.

We slept exposed. It was midday. It was another year. We thought of our marriage days. Of the child we had in August. He ate peaches and pretended nothing would ever change. And then we looked at one another and it was many years later. From someone else's window, we heard the music we used to listen to. We meditated on whether to keep the one chair we had, since we were two and there was just one chair. We looked at life, hour after hour as if it were growing. And then I turned around, placed my hand on Javier's heart—suddenly a cry. We had waited too long to start.

The Other Woman

I say, no perfume
no open windows
no cooking, no waiting
I say, on any
layover, go to the
airport bathroom, leave
the bracelet he gave you.
Get a house in the suburbs
have a whiskey or
a gin and tonic,
find a scapegoat for your sins.
I say, the texture of your hair
is rough, the fabric
of your clothes tacky,
the fog in your eyes a dangerous bridge.
I say, stop coming for him—
I forbid him to come to you.
In you is a basement without lights
a place with an accent he recognizes,
maybe loves. *No*, the other woman
finally responds, *he only loves his absence*
and whatever is left of him is mine—
I'll kill myself, she continues.
And I wonder if he asks her to say that.

Why Men Die Young

1

Because they can't stop dancing when they should be sleeping
Because they listen to Fleetwood Mac when the president's speaking
Because they buy houses they can't afford
and cars with names they can't pronounce
Because they are reckless when caution is necessary
Because they are obsessed with freedom when they have no money
and obsessed with money when they have a lot of it
Because they ask for mercy only when they've run out of options
and imagine love only to count the tulips they left dying
Because they have no clue what the latter means
That's the trouble with men—they are lightheaded even on holidays.

2

When a man finally finds his love's bed and silently buries his face in her breasts, their flesh motionless in an unexplored hour, her hips rising, her nipples hard, her eyes widening into an opening he cannot see, her breathing escalating, a soft moaning, and he remains still, he realizes that before people wake, behind shaken minds and closed doors, minutes pass without apology and men walk unsatisfied besides bodies seeking each other.

3

They await anxiously
what Eros will tell them
about who they are

when they're not craving
for what they will find out
after they've divided earth,
and when they discover their language
is where their bodies fail to be,
they let fire fill their mouths.

Scènes dans une Chambre Mauve

La Première

I look at every one of your toes
and touch them carefully
with my index finger,

I ask you to scratch the sky,
ask you to faint when I place my lips
on yours and then I tell you
that if you come toward me
without falling,
bite my neck while
I scream your name,
I will tie you up
and let you go.

La Troisème

You make me give you my hairpins,
ask me to describe what I am feeling—
like night with a different face.

You pass your fingers down my lower back,
grab me and find your way to the closest
part of me—the curtain tight,
the ceiling shrinking,
pleasure beating the air,
and you wondering who is torturing whom.

Les Après

We take green apple from the wooden bowl,
cut it into tiny pieces—what better way
to feel alive in someone else's room?

In Jerusalem

He walks in as if he knows exactly where he is going to sit, his hair well combed, jet, with some strokes of white, I try not to look at him but he comes over and asks, *Who are you*, I don't answer, he is embarrassed, but not enough, he says, *Tell me your name*, I still don't answer, he buys his coffee, orders a salmon sandwich, bends over to see the pine tree outside, I feel him moving closer, I try not to look at him but can't help it, he is now suddenly shy, and that intrigues me, I wonder if his name is Ari or Haythem, wonder who owned this old house turned into Café Aroma, did a bride get dressed here, did a young girl lose her virginity here, exactly where we are sitting, him and I, maybe I was his mistress and he made me wear a black skirt, a white transparent blouse, a gold shoe that I borrowed, slightly too tight too tall too narrow, and then he asks me to sit at the edge of the couch, I think, *No*, but never say it, we look at each other, a small smile, a tune of Abdel Wahab in Hebrew playing, who will save us now, the music gets louder, the words clearer, the voice unfamiliar, I promise to keep my hair long, to continue to wait for the key to the door, we watch the god between us reveal a secret, we already had the time to imagine our kiss, already had the time to say *Illalika*, until we meet again, then I realize I have to ask him, *what street are we on*, he never answers, that's how I find out his name and the inevitable, maybe it will all end when nothing can interrupt the conversation we are having with the mirror we've borrowed from each other.

Les Éventails, Portraits of Passion

The shadows of birds fading on a fighter's back

The undressing of words on an unstamped postcard

The wet swings in the distant park

The jealousy of raindrops on the umbrella of lovers

The laughter of a boy before a bird

The song of two flutes, two swords, two bracelets, two fingers

The stare of a wave before a pearl

The yearning between the legs of a farmer's wife

The opening of doors   closing midday

The sudden howling of our muse—and

les éventails—disturbing the guest inside of us

The Bulgarian Orchestra

You touch my dimples
after the first aria,
tell me what you are about to do
when the music is at its highest.
Nineteen beats before
you finish describing
where we will enter,
nineteen beats before
your throat gets dry
and your eyes turn a shade of red,
nineteen beats before
you put your hands under my skirt,
nineteen beats before
the walls get wet,
nineteen beats before our fall,
we move deep into what
we will do to each other.

Carrousel, or After Lovemaking

II

Sometimes I thought I liked
your crimson lips.
Sometimes I thought
your dark-water compass
was mine.
Then I saw the rust
you kept in your apartment,
the bees outside your door,
your half-painted toenails,
the pedal on your chest
taking all the air out.
I heard the harp-weavers
around you
demanding you withhold the music,
strings with the dried blood
of those we are unable to name,
and I thought, who are we?
I realized we had both
sleepwalked into
a room of horns.

I

I will never die or love enough, you warned.
I didn't believe you. And I was right.
The storms inside you turned into music.
Some intruders became your lovers
but most you chased away.
Stooped beside a basket of cactus,
beside sheets of papyrus,
we spent time in half-prayers,
fooling around with happiness
as we hummed the records we no longer played,
looked at photos from our old cameras,
and heard the giggling inside.

You turned off the oil lamp—
all we wanted
was a new way of finding birth, a slow dance, a carrousel.

In January, *Amor y Lluvia*

¡Oh vida!, ¿me reservas por ventura algún don?

Amado Nervo, "The Gift"

This is how we met—
one evening, there was noise in the square,
books in our hands, a quiet lusting
                    (We really met at a bar)

There was light on both sides of our shadows;
we were lost in lucid dream
                    (We were drunk)

We sang, held hands, nothing like this
ever happened to us before,
we were alive in each other's voice
                    (We forgot what we spoke about)

We kissed at 1 a.m.:
it was a still night
                    (Until the bartender yelled, *Last call*)

We told each other, but not out loud:
*The more we develop our own sensibility, the more ironically
we know ourselves*

                    (Certainly, we agreed with Pessoa, even if we
                    never discussed it)

We left together that night not knowing that
we would lie on the bed, inseparable,
an open window, snow waiting to tell us

to love harder, because what we wanted most was each other
                    (He thought, *This is it or heartbreak*; I was thinking the
                    same)

We left together not knowing that weeks later
I would be looking at him standing on a wooden chair,
his jeans on, his red belt undone, his shirt off,
trying to hang a curtain on an uneven window frame
                    (He almost fell, and we laughed, laughed some more
                    when I said, *You are neither earth nor man.*)

Then by the dripping faucet we kissed
by the record player he described as magic we kissed
We wondered if God had a right hand
                    (Yes, we had those thoughts)

We spoke of what moves
bitter cherries on the floor and cried;
we spoke of the trumpet and the twilight,
of the ballad of the Irish horses—
yes, the love of horses runs through Irish blood
and he was an Irishman
                    (I thought I was too—who doesn't want to be in the
                    company of Beckett, Yeats, and Roddy Doyle, though
                    of course, I would never abandon Darwish)

We spoke of red white and blue, and our embrace,
of the walk we took on the beach,
the old bottle of wine we opened,
and I thought, wider than quiet or noise, is his voice

We saw each other at the edge of the ocean,
and the word, his eyes, our lips

the mystery he placed inside of me—
childlike and unfolding in my sleep—
is a gift—about belonging,
watching snowflakes cover our shoes

To my January 20th

Lubhyati: Love Letters

Yesterday

Dearest Love,
I can still see the red blossoms inside your eyes, the petals around you,
the crickets not far from you. Where will you be when we reach the soft
cry beneath a parachute?

Last night I dreamed we were young. Your brown hair on your forehead,
your brown eyes open wide, and your back slightly arched. I had a red
parasol; you, a black fleece. I imagined holding you at a garden party or
late at night when everyone pretends to sleep. And then I found a note
that started with, *He desires.* . . . the rest was torn away.

Today

Love,
Who have you slept with over the years? Maybe that Kashmiri—her
naked body pressed against you to prevent you the space to see another.
But Aishwarya, with lips too pink to resist took you into her pavilion.
Her legs demanded obedience. You allowed her everything until the night
you could no longer think of her breast. Her loud cries. Her mouth.
The cold around you. And then came Abha, Priya, Aditi, Padma, Radha,
and Sanjana. But only when we did cartwheel after cartwheel did you
find the limited edition of that book we both own.

Yesterday

Dearest Love,
Describe the images that torture your sleep. The trees that grow against stony walls. You cannot. Because you are nowhere. Have flown off with the weight of your sadness and sixty bags of dust. And you no longer fear dying in the fog fading in your mind, in the crowd of black smoke, after the stroke of an old clock. Between our words, what's wrong defines itself. And we sink into what we smuggled inside of us—notes tied to the shadows of bats.

Today

Dear Love,
The orchard keeper is gone. Did you know? He knew the history of the sky so well, and that of the clouds too. And I keep wondering, does it matter who breathes where? He still breathes all over the small cabin by the lake. He used to polish his shoes every hour. And paint—watercolor. Did you know? Now he says he is going to be a saxophone player. And you, who will you become after desire?

Yesterday

Dearest Love,
I did not realize that somewhere in the sand or the mud lay the terrible grief of a fool. Yes, Tagore is dead. His collectibles—cavern photos, knives, seashells—have been buried with him. What he left behind: the slice of bread he never ate, the pond he forgot to name. So my love, which would you choose, grass or snow? The slowness of maidens as they sing or hard flesh against a rock of ice? Answer soon— if you desire.

Undated

It was nighttime. It was May 5th, 7 p.m. Exactly. We took our clothes off. You kissed the birthmark under my arm—the only person who ever noticed it. We wanted to trace all that we had lost, the details: the flickering green bulb in the room we imagined making love in, the green feathers on the bed, their impeccable silence, the messages about the snow-covered fields and the short skirt you insisted I wear. We listened to prayers in Bengali, French, Arabic, Greek, and Hindi, then hurried to the next room to recite everything we heard. The hissing of waterfalls, the joining of echoes under gray skies. We never took our clothes off. We needed each other too much.

Love and Strange Horses—*Elegía Erótica*

A horse. A stranger. An anthem. An impossible thereafter.

A lonely rift. A grove of trees. A touch. A cry. A murmur.

In what hours do lovers arrive?

In what hour did mine arrive?

How deep must he be touched to enter?

How deep must he enter to touch?

My lips. Body. Flesh. The curve of my neck.

Come on my flag. On my name. On the tip of my voice.

Horse. Stranger. Anthem.

This love is behind us. In front of us.

This is the bed. Sheet. Table. This is the room, empty.

Or is this now, an elegy to strange horses,

an erotica slipping into a body of questions.

III

Movement Three—Terre Música

A bird stood there—it said something ambiguous.

Yannis Ritsos, "Geographic Origins"

El Mundo

The first came on a white horse, the second on a red horse, the third on a black horse, the fourth on a pale horse, the four horsemen of the apocalypse came, and one after the other everything vanished, the rabbits left, the tigers left, the grass gone dry, the birds left, the butterflies left, the sky gone black, and Arvak gone, the crickets left, the giraffes left, and Balios gone, the water left, the leaves and the owls left, and Black Bess gone, the west wind left, the south wind left, and Shibdiz and Dinos gone, the eagles left, the merchants left, and Grani gone, the deers left, the gazelles left, and Haizum gone, the cavebirds left, the wolfwatchers left, and Lampton and Sleipnir gone, but the Vedic Horse Sacrifice reminds us of the erotic spring fertility rite, of Veruna, of the magic the world can possess, of the horseshoe protecting us, of St. Martine, St. Maurice, St. George, and St. Victor and of Borak.

Four Horsemen of the Apocalypse: in The Revelation of St. John the Divine, four agents of destruction, two being agents of war and two of famine and pestilence (100, Cooper).

Arvak: in Norse mythology, the horse that draws the sun's chariot, driven by the maiden Sol; Balios: one of the horses given by Neptune to Peleus, which later belonged to Achilles; Black Bess: mythical mare, created by Harrison Ainsworth in *Rookwood*, which carried Dick Turpin from London to York; Shibdiz: the Persian Bucephalus, fleeter than the wind; charger of Chosroes II; Dinos: the marvel, Diomedes' horse; Grani: gray-colored, Siegfried's horse of marvelous swiftness; Haizum: the horse of the archangel Gabriel in the Koran; Lampton: the bright one; Sleipnir, Odin's eight-footed gray horse that could traverse both land and sea and typifies the wind that blows from the eight principal points. (131–32)

The Vedic Horse Sacrifice is possibly the oldest and most famous. The animal was greatly venerated by the Aryans and the sacrifice was attended by the king and queen with four hundred attendants; the occasion was an erotic spring fertility rite. There is also Veruna, god of the waters, as the Cosmic Horse and when Vishnu appears for the tenth and last time at the end of this era it will be as Kalki, a white horse (130).

In Islam, the horse is "God sent" and the Prophet was carried to heaven by the steed Borak (131).

In Christian art, the horse is held to represent courage and generosity. It is an attribute of St. Martine, St. Maurice, St. George and St. Victor, all of whom are represented on horseback (131).

Cooper, J. C., ed. *Brewer's Book of Myth and Legend*. Oxford: Cassell Publishers Ltd, 1992.

The Meadows

Lover, you leave *want* even on chairs, murmur words in languages you
    don't know.

You play chess.

Wrap the only melody left around you, knock back the only whiskey
    left from the blue glass, and let your body sway in mid-air
    so that the wind can run its breath on your neck.

And so it all begins, the way it leaves, with a sliding, a spilling of paint
    on lust.

Now your eyes have gone blank.

The birds around you have gone to another awakening.

The mules are smaller, slower.

The music is faster, and circling around danger.

Your mind is throbbing, wondering if what you took, will last.

And you resent those who have found a way to question the living
    properly.

You touch yourself to remember the meadows, what they felt like
    inside you.

The Song Fox

And then there is time—
a string of features,
nothing more than
a continued hush

and then there is
the swelling inside,
an immeasurable
distance to desire

and then
the glistening of the river
against a shadow
that could be ours

and then we tell ourselves
it's safe to believe in nothing
except the fox's song,
which we never remember.

Hayat

There is order in what
is lovely,
she thought,

she for whom the day remained sad,
a room full of beautiful objects, like the mirror from
Al Quds, the ceramic vase from Hebron,

she for whom the day neglected light
and hopeless pleasure,
like a voice cutting itself
to sing.

There is order in what
remains irresistible
and broken
and light and full of strokes.

Then she asks,
Was there order
in what I collected
on afternoons
when the boys
drew their faces
under their chins
above their hearts?

Yes, an order for their end.
Now, they bring her apples in the dark.

White Trees

When the white trees are no longer in sight
they are telling us something,
like the body that undresses
when someone is around,
like the woman who wants
to read what her nude curves
are trying to say,
of what it was to be together,
lips on lips
but it's over now, the town
we once loved in, the maps
we once drew, the echoes that
once passed through us
as if they needed something we had.

Here and There

Perhaps there will always be struggle—maybe we cannot imagine dreaming as another person dreams. That the movements of our hearts, in both intimate and public spaces, are real only to those who think they are surreal, surreal only to those who think they are real. Fiction or truth—which one is myth? The eyes at every intersection doubt. The rain anticipates. The road contemplates. Is it possible to open these gates?

We are unable to walk faster but will arrive, even if it takes a long time.

When what is invisible dies and we pretend not to know, we die too.

Isn't freedom purity and perdition at the same time?

Fear. The night. The incomprehension. The mystery. Poetry awaking in us—a miracle. A startling. A sudden revelation or wonder. What truly makes us afraid? What brings us closer?

Perhaps what breathes around us is only shadow or symbol.

Who is god to us?

Should we long for interludes?

But isn't it time to meet?

Back home, a wall. A cracked heart. And all the movements of that heart like the olive trees that ploy truth.

The mist is real.

Did you know?

It's here and there.

The Songmaker—19 Arabics

World is crazier and more of it than we think,
Incorrigibly plural. I peel and portion
A tangerine and spit the pips and feel
The drunkenness of things being various.

On the tongue on the eyes on the ears in the palms of one's hands—
There is more than glass between the snow and the huge roses.

Louis MacNeice

Which one of us is free
—he asks his violin,
as he tunes its strings—
you or I?

Which past or present do I choose,
which exile do you remember,
which bedroom did I leave you in,
under which lemon tree did I compose 19 *Arabics*:
Yesterday I carried Hob Hawa Hadb Harara Hanan Huyam Jawa
to the border, and waited.
Today, I stood by Tahabbub Tahannoun Taraffouq Tatayyum Wajd
    Walah
at the crossing, and waited.
Tomorrow, I will accompany Danaf Gharam Shaghaf Mawaddah
    Oulfa Ouns
to where death sits, and wait.
As for tonight, I will think of the nineteen ways I wait.

Where are the olive trees
why can't I see the almond tree
or the sun
a wall hiding the light even from my shadow.

Is there a bridge anywhere?

We return to a certain love or love to a certain return.

Are you tired? You look tired.

Tell me which holy book is on your shelf
—all of them—
it's language that keeps the land as it should be.

I forgot to ask,
when the glassblower and
the woman with
bells around her ankle
distracted,
said, *Sabah Alkhayr,*
did you answer,

Did you?

Am I the songmaker
or are you?

Answer.

Which bird did I speak to
when we marched together,
beyond—
myth after myth?

Who said we need to be strangers,
when we listen to the same music?

Interview with Jesus or Edward Hopper

Shut it not up I beseech thee, do not shut up these
usual yet hidden things from my desire.
Augustine, *Confessions* XI

—*What message did you deliver?*
That the universe was covered with a shroud.

—*What color did you use?*
The ones nature forgot to present.

—*What shapes fascinated you most?*
The ones under any tower bridge.

—*What intrigued you?*
An imagined body, crowded with light.

—*What did you find unbearable?*
Jesus, when I lost him.

—*Why are confessions so intriguing?*
They are?

—*Why draw, paint?*
Because it illuminates
even when you are not looking,

and St. Augustine is in my chest
unable to decide if outside he can see

the spaces still undivided by the world.

Winter Phantoms

They say a prayer
in the kingdom of Antony
and behind the walls of Cleopatra.

They say a prayer
as farmers conspire, convicts fantasize,
as a shepherd gets caught in a windmill,
and a bullfighter holds his drumbeats tight
in the country of lost warriors.

They say a prayer
by lamps where
men sleep with different women,
lips the color of plum.

But can they feel the pain of others
as leaves tremble in their hands,
as winter comes and stays—
what's in the broken pieces of earth
as the human face crumbles in the attic.

Portraits & Truths

Palmira: I am not mistress of myself, and how
Can I be thine?

Voltaire, *Mahomet*, 1714

Anath
Canaanite goddess of love

She is the one holding
on to the rail and
waiting for any destination

Astrild
Norse god of erotic love

He is the one suspended
in an ancient city where
glow abandons paradise

Astlik
Armenian goddess of love, fertility

She is a row of sorrows
behind
a river of wrecked gallows

Hora
Roman goddess of beauty

She is the one that searches
songbooks for
missing braids

Ix Chel
Mayan goddess of sexual relations

She is by the tree by the window
about to reach the orchard
but gets distracted

Tammuz
Mesopotamian god of fertility

He is like happiness
missing
his heartbeats

Kilya

Inca goddess of marriage

She is the one who knows
that solitude and paradise
are ghost towns of fading skies

Antheia

Greek goddess of love, flowers

She sculpts the gardens
forgetting she has inherited
the roots of trees

Godx

Origin Unknown

I am the one who belongs nowhere, the one who misses these portraits most.

Black Butterflies, A Lost Tango

I thought I'd find my heart / where I'd kept your eyes two brown butterflies . . . /
The sun shall be covered by us / the sun in our eyes for ever covered /
with black butterflies.

Ingrid Jonker, "I searched for my own heart"
and "I drift in the wind"

Nine is the number to remember
The magic to be close to
Three times three equals nine
Three we must all pray for
Three owls, three fences, three lives
And nineteen is the infinite
Black butterflies on crosses
Crossing trees
Trees bowing to shadows
Shadows crowding heaven
Heaven falling ninety miles an hour
Hours, a wind full of curses
Curses, underwater
Water, a necessary weight
Weight, like books pressing against broken ribs
Ribs, wounds gone through us only
To hit the one we detest.
Now the tango is lost . . .
∞

. . . The hills are disappearing
Hills with their smooth grass
Grass with fall's yellow leaves on top

Leaves under trees
Trees, with pigeons, birds, crows
Crows, holding the silhouette of night
Night, a colony of stardust
Stars, like small holes in the universe
Universe, rows of bolts
Bolts, that disappear
That cry, *have mercy*
We all need the doves
Whispers drawing life
From nothing
The gods in us disappointed
And we still haven't read Corinthians
Still haven't asked
About the river gliding
Its origin
If solitude is
Our way to grieve
Where are the black butterflies
As we braid our sadness to their wings?

Les Cloîtres

Christian looked after Les Cloîtres,
a monastery, where the trees and mist
were words for sermons. He recited verses
like blessings on every inch of this place.
He especially loved the different ways
the branches chiseled in the air.
Then Isabelle came. She fell in love with him.
She thought he was enlightened—
his calm, his devotion. They declared their affections
at zero degrees. But as the years went by,
she realized he would never love her
as he loved the grounds she found him on.
So she left. He didn't understand. But she returned soon after.
She bought Les Cloîtres. He realized at that point how much
she loved him. She had gone to make sure
the place always belonged to him.
But when she said, *you have to leave,* he said nothing.
She waited for his anger, smiled—had her revenge on him.
He walked the place all night, his love immovable. He smiled.
She found him the next day under a blossoming tree.
He died sitting up, his legs straight—the shape of his victory.

White Strawberries

It's disturbing not to like white strawberries,
she tells him, *not to know they are from Chile.*

Then she wears her red dress, red net stockings,
red lipstick and tells him about the forest outside,

tells him how he will find lightning
in the curves of their kiss,

how the lake stretches south to north,
how the blackberries will grow around their bodies.

She tells him she wants him
when he watches grasshoppers in the wild grass,

the dragonfly, the oak tree and the cold stream passing,
and she sees his eyes against a rushing silence.

She explains how she invented his voice for years.
Then one day he asks her, *do you like what you hear?*

She responds, *it's life,*
it disturbs—

it's disturbing you don't like white strawberries.

Sailing to Tarsus

Misfortune does not lessen however much you speak of it.
But there are pains that will not stay quiet in the heart.
Cavafy, "A Love"

I hear you every evening,
a question, then another.
We have been fools.
Have gone to hidden ruins.
Violet yellows.
Have kept photos of where
the Trojans once stood,
where the horses of Achilles
once passed through,
to remember what
we both like.
Held on to the word Riza,
and never listened
to "Travma" loud enough.
Now, we can't return to
our stare looming in a bluesy field,
but I still imagine telling you
about my dream:
eating chocolate, vanilla, strawberry,
and lemon sorbet with you.
I will sail until underneath
the tremble of the sea
(something to do with love)
there is saltwater on your tongue.

To Panagiota

Dream of O'Keeffe's Dream

Prophet in Flowers

Under the leaves of winter
the icy glare of heartache
a wishing moon, its gray shades
trying to keep the circle
of yellow beam intact
like an opening against the sky
like the hand of a prophet
telling us to imagine a secret

Red and Pink

Outside a valley of red mist
and pink clouds, hanging—
waiting for a sign
of anything—
I ask you what
you are doing—
you say,
opening an umbrella

Blue Quiver

I know the ending:
two words making love
a quivering
two bodies unable to sweat
moonlight afraid of prayers

flying in the nightmares of sinners
a fence of sorrow   a dove on our chest
waiting to be summoned
a sentence
unable to begin

Glassblower

There are days when he knows
the song Moses sang,
the distance between the orchard
and the post office, when he could carry
a book as if it were a lover not a rival,
read its marvels not its errors, memorize its poems
not its titles, hold its echoes, bite into them
as if they were succulent peaches,
and there are days he finds
crushed glass under his feet

Rain on Whispers

Morning—
a buried rain of whispers,
a thousand birds
wondering if they will
awaken in a blue symphony
or remain abandoned
on a Persian wall

Midnight—
like the remorse of low tides,
wondering if it will apologize

when asked: *Is it over?*
Realize it has forgiven
truth for lying

Black Door in Desert

The desert heat
the wanderer nodding off
his shirt wet with sweat
his breathing heavy—
he must have known many women
but never loved,
you could tell by the way a man sleeps
if he's ever loved.
He is not still.
But what would I know
when he moved forward
I pushed him back to fix my shirt

Metamorphosis

Raindrops rest on the ladder
by the moon
We tear the pieces of the day
leave the black hats we have collected
by the red hill
We hold the water jar tight
and push out
our grief.
We are the suspension
we believe in

Sky Above Clouds, Walk into Horizon

He delivers,
The Equivalent—
a special dark
where every inch
is a sequence of dreams.
But is it water or sky?
It doesn't matter, he says.

I said it differently.

19 Harbors

He travels under a low sky
she can't see but knows
he moves when she moves.

Something close to him
hides his limping voice, hides
what he is too hungry to become.

He loves her. Looks at her for
three minutes. Kisses her for four
and looks at her again
for forty-four seconds.

He says: cover your breast.
Uncover your top. Open your blouse.
Untie your hair. Scream *I want you.*
Pull your pants down. Put mine on.
Then let your neck tilt to the right.
To the left. So a tide with ice
might find you.

Where are you, he asks.
Looking for the harbors, she says,
now that the sea has
tumbled nineteen times.

Love and Strange Horses — *Terre Música*

Because we no longer heard the hoofs of horses,
Because we no longer saw them galloping, no longer saw
them standing on the coral shore, we asked,
where does the music of the human voice hide?

Can you find its song
in the sea, uncertain of its waters,
in the field, uncertain of its hay,
in the cherry blossom, uncertain of its soil,
between miles of fallen trunks,
or perhaps in the freeze after the heat?

Because we no longer saw what is holy and wet,
because we called the Titans and the horse thieves
and the only message they sent back was:
In the end, nature will be
roaring, drowning, ruining, ruling,
we asked, can we dare love to find
the legend abandoned in música
as grass reaches out for our weeping.

Notes

"Flames at Hurr Mountain": *Hurr* means "free" in Arabic.

"Love and Strange Horses—Intima'": *Intima'* means "belonging" in Arabic.

"Lubhyati: Love Letters": *Lubhyati* means "he desires" in Sanskrit.

"El Mundo": The footnotes in this poem are taken, almost verbatim, from J. C. Cooper, ed., *Brewer's Book of Myth and Legend* (Oxford: Cassel Publishers Ltd., 1992).

"Hayat": *Hayat* means "life" in Arabic.

"The Songmaker—*19 Arabics*": In Arabic, *Hob, Hawa, Hadb, Harara, Hanan, Huyam, Jawa, Tahabbub, Tahannoun Taraffouq, Tatayyum, Wajd, Walah, Danaf, Gharam, Shaghaf, Mawaddah, Oulfa, Ouns,* all mean love or a variation of love; *Sabah Alkhayr* means good morning.

"Interview with Jesus or Edward Hopper": Augustine, *Confessions* XI, as rendered by Anne Carson in "Evening Wind."

"Running Horses" by Gita Meh (cover painting): The artist explains that her Running Horses Series was inspired by the Quran, Verse 100, Running Horses, which says: "I take witness the breathless and panting horses, I take witness the horses that make sparks of fire with their hoofs, I swear to horses of early morning, running together and make dust rise into the air covering the morning breeze, I take the horses as my witness that human beings are not thankful to their creator and they know it themselves. They love money and other immediate family only above all. Don't they know that after death all shall come to life and all stored in their hearts will come to reality and that God is aware of their inner intentions?"

Acknowledgments

Sincere thanks to the editors and staff of the following publications in which the following poems previously appeared, sometimes in earlier versions:

Atlas ("Akhmatova and I: Boleros," "Elephant Fever," and "Sun Moon Midnight"); *Barrow Street* ("The Other Woman"); *Callaloo* ("Of the End"); *Drunken Boat* 10 ("Corriendo" and "Winter Phantoms"); *Language for a New Century: Contemporary Poetry from the Middle East, Asia and Beyond* ("Autobiography of Night"); *New Quest* ("The Hawk Quartet," "The Song Fox," and "White Trees"); *PBS NewsHour's Artbeat* ("Brokenmusic," "Intermisión" and "Love and Strange Horses—*Terre Música*"); *Sirena: Poesía Arte y Crítica/Poetry Art and Criticism* ("Corriendo"); *Urhalpool* ("Sailing to Tarsus"); *Virginia Quarterly Review* ("Listen, Tonight").

⌒

Edward, you have been great light in my life, there aren't enough ways to say thank you. Rina Montalvo, gracias amiga por hacer el sueño posible.

I would like to thank my parents, my sister, Alexandra, and my brother, Dimitri for always being there for me. Many thanks to my dear friends Danielle Balest Georgaklis and Pamela Georgiadis Wolf—Ειοαι μεοα στη καρδια μου.

Deepest gratitude to Tina Chang, Ravi Shankar, Tony Barnstone, Sholeh Wolpé, Ed Pavlic, Sarah Jane Freyman, Suzanne Roberts, Rana Kazkaz, Ram Devineni, Ellen Peckham, AE Ventures for the Fellowship, the amazing team at Pittsburgh University Press, and especially Yusef Komunyakaa, Subhi Hadidi, and David Groff for believing in me and supporting my work. And a special thanks to Ed Ochester for his guidance and friendship throughout the years.

And to you Michael, who came into my life, and changed everything.